NEVAEH

Published and distributed by
Heather Bell and Gregg Noel

DEDICATION
To the glory of God for the gift of poetry.
To my mother for her inspiring love.
To my husband and children who have encouraged
and supported me through the years.
To my beloved son David who is now in the arms of Jesus.

Dedicated to David

A Mothers Love For Her Son

I was kneeling in intensive care
Praying for my son
Holding both his hands in mine
And saying, "God's will be done".
I talked to him about Jesus
And the forgiveness He can give
And as the tears rolled down my face
Jesus took him home to live
I knew the angels carried him
In their tender loving care
And as I said my last goodbye
Jesus answered a mother's prayer.

Page Index

P1:	My Mother My Friend	P25:	Your Throne Room
	For Taking and Forgiving	P26:	My soul was lost
P2:	Incarcerated Whisper	P27:	Help Me Show My Friends
P3:	Forgive Me Lord		The Gifts Of God
	Morning Had Broken	P28:	As I Pass Through This World Lord
P4:	I Shall Come Home Again	P29:	Many Religions
	Life Is For Living	P30:	He Grows With Me
P5:	When I Didn't Know You Lord		Jesus My Brother
P6:	Stop Calling	P31:	Be prepared for an Angel
P7:	If Jesus Came		To See the Stars Shine Above
	A Whisper of Love	P32:	Resting on your shoulders
P8:	You Are My Fortress My Rock		The Lord Understands
	Calm me with Your Spirit	P33:	Anointed Hands
P9:	Cherished and Blessed		Praise God In All You Do
	As I Sit By The River	P34:	Ask For Forgiveness
P10:	Before I Knew Your Holy Name		Teach Me How To Live
	Take A Stand	P35:	The Lord Is On Your Side
P11:	Spiritually Minded	P36:	The Face of Jesus
	Jesus Be With Me		Happy times
P12:	In my Father's house there are	P37:	Joseph's Dedication
	many mansions	P38:	The River
	Hold my hand lord	P39:	Thy Wondrous Love
P13:	Trust and Believe		Happiness
	Don't despair	P40:	When I'm alone
P14:	His Hand in Mine		Rainbow
P15:	My Healer		Plan and Purpose
	Shield of faith	P41:	Matthew 18:10
	Thankyou Jesus		Never Ending Story
P16:	The power of prayer	P42:	I'm A little light for Jesus
	Shine the light through me	P43:	Multicolored angels
P17:	A Father and Son		Anointed Hands
P18:	Be my strength when I'm lonely Lord	P44:	Guardian Angels
P19:	The Lords prayer		My Rock
P20:	Wisdom	P45:	Good Morning Jesus
	Underneath your wing		You and Me
P21:	Angels	P46:	If I were a Bird
	Praise Glory and Honor	P47:	Mould Me Lord
P22:	Happiness		Lord Jesus How I Love Thee
	Jesus will see me through	P48:	The Miracle of Birth
P23:	In the beginning	P49:	My Precious Daughter
P24:	There's power in Jesus name		You are so worthy to be Praised
	Under Gods wings	P50:	Flowers In Gods Garden

P51:	I Love You So	P82:	My Everything
	No Past		Watch and Pray
P52:	I Give You My life	P83:	You are the way
	You Understand		Patiently wait
P53:	Love God Your Father	P84:	Early Morn
P54:	How would we be?		My Friend
	Thank You Lord For Me	P85:	This is the day
P55:	I Feel So Great		You are my Lord
P56/57:	Australia Remember	P86:	Your Creation
P58/59:	I Am The Murray		Help me Lord
P60:	Australia My Land	P87:	To my sister's
P61:	Reserve Us A Seat	P88:	You created all
P62:	Bless me in my home Lord		When I am lonely
P63:	Hear my Prayer	P89:	Be still my child
	One of a kind		Home to rest
P64:	Beacon of Light	P90:	Take my hand
P65:	Faith		Become my child
	The Foot of Your Throne	P91:	Bless me today Lord
P66:	Hear My Father	P92:	Sermon on the Mount
	He'll See You Through		Jesus Takes Our Burden
P67:	My Pen My Friend	P93:	Water of life
	Sunlight Through The Cube	P94:	He walks with me
P68:	Look For The Butterflies		Angels
P69:	Love	P95:	Just Suppose
P70:	Create in me your Spirit	P96:	Reach Out To Jesus
	Trust in me		Speak to me my child
P71:	Sow Our Father's Seeds	P97:	Give him the Glory
	He Grows With Me	P98:	Jesus be with me
P72:	Life is a Blessing	P99:	The gospel of love
	Faith and Hope	P100:	Treasures in Heaven
P73:	I'm not Alone		Communion
	Praise	P101:	Man And Wife
P74:	Death is just a whisper	P102:	Poem Of Communion
	Butterfly	P103:	Thank You For Making Me
P75:	When I Go Don't Cry For Me		
P76:	Angel Wings (Scott's song)		
P77:	Wisdom And Knowledge		
	Under Your Wing		
P78:	Jesus Knows Our Needs		
	You Are Mine		
P79:	Troubled Waters		
	Never Ending Journey		
P80:	Don't Cry No More		
P81:	Do Unto Others		

Mum's Poem for David

David is so special to me
He is not just a son but a friend
He's the mirror of my soul
And the reflection of my heart
And our friendship will never end
I know that right now we're apart for awhile
But our love links the breaks in the chain
And two little roses sent from above
Healed my heart that was full of pain
I know now there are things we cannot change
No matter how hard we try
A broken heart can never heal
If we spend each day asking why
We have to learn to accept God's way
For life needs sunshine and rain
And if I looked through the mirror of my soul
David would say "Mum, don't cry again
Be happy for me, for I love you so
Thank you for taking the time to pray
Just think of me Mum and the love we shared
And know that I am not far away."

DAVID'S POEMS TO ME
My Mother My Friend

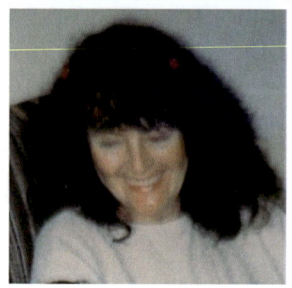

She can change my moods from tears to laughter
She tells me about love and the life there after
She's what keeps the family together
She forgives you always and loves you forever
She smiles constantly, her smile to me has no end
She's my mother, she's my friend ❤️

For Taking and Forgiving

For taking and forgiving
And for playing the game
For praying for my future
In the days that remain
For giving the rain
When I'm feeling so dry
For giving me the answers
When I'm asking you why
And my oh my for that I love you

Incarcerated Whisper

The sunsets far away
As the moon ends another day
Goes unseen through our own confusions
Alone I sit on an empty hill
Where for a moment time stood still
Captured freely in a living dream
Distant echoes of a mountain stream
High above the sky
Beneath the stars a cloud glides by,
Out of the shadows nothing is real
They will never know how I feel
David John Bell

Forgive Me Lord

Forgive me lord of all my sins
Even the ones I don't know
Let your love for others
Through me flow
Give me grace and mercy to
Let me forgive others
The way you do
I love you so much for dying for me
For taking my place at cavalry
Now I am washed as clean as snow
Thankyou Jesus
Only you know

Morning Had Broken

Morning had broken
Not a word spoken
I looked at you and you looked back
My heart was choking and that's a fact
So, till we reunite
Not maybe or might
I'll treasure the memories that we feel
The love between mother and son
Is all very real

I Shall Come Home Again

I shall come home again
Home after the waiting
The waiting with longing
And maddened with dreaming
I shall come home again

Life is for Living

Life is for living
So let us live.
Life is for giving
So let us give.
Life is for sharing
So let us share.
Life is for caring
So let us care.
Life is Jesus
Who is God's Son.
Life is the victory,
Through Jesus we've won.

When I didn't know You Lord

When I didn't know You Lord
And did not have Your mark,
All my fear and troubles Lord
Came to meet me in the dark.

But now I live in You Lord
And You are here in me,
I have no fears and troubles Lord
Your light has set me free.

I know Your love, I know Your power,
I know how great You are.
You're in my home, You're at my work,
You're with me in my car.

Lord what was I before You came?
My footsteps they were slow.
I had such fear and doubt and shame,
Oh Lord, I know you know.

You came and made my footsteps light
And quick to spread Your name.
You took away my fear and doubt
And left me without shame.

And I will never leave you Lord,
Oh never, never, never.
And I will always love You Lord
Forever and ever and ever.

Stop Calling

Stop calling! Stop calling!
I have plenty of time.
I'll come when I'm ready.
I have my whole life to live.

Stop calling! Stop calling!
I'm not ready for you yet.
I'm having too good time.
I have my friends to consider
What would they say?
If all of a sudden, I started to pray.

Stop calling! Stop calling!
I know you're there.
But I don't need you just yet.
Maybe later on when I'm older
And my life is slipping by.
There's time enough to give your way a try.

Stop calling! Stop calling!
I'm not really bad.
I have all my friends
I give to charities
I help where I can
Why make me a part of Your plan?

Wait, what's happening, I'm falling, it's very dark.
I remember I was driving
Oh no the car, the accident,
I can't hear Your calling anymore, please wait.
It's all over, I'm too late.

If Jesus came

What would you do if Jesus came
Again to heal the blind and lame?
Would you believe the things you saw
And would you follow and adore
Someone who said, "I am God's Son."?
Or would you turn your back and run
When all Our Saviour wanted to say was
"I am the truth, the life, the way."
To hear from His stories true
Where there's a message for me and you.
Sometimes we listen but never hear
Only believe Him, do not fear.

A Whisper of Love

Death is just a whisper
Of God saying, "My child come home
Your time on earth is over
And I've prepared for You a home
I am waiting here to thank you
For spreading My Son's Name
You've been a good and faithful servant
Since in your life He came
So, one day you'll hear my whisper
And the gates will be open wide
And all the ones you ever loved
Will be waiting for You inside"

You are My Fortress My Rock

You are my fortress, my rock, my guide
When fear comes upon me in you I hide
In darkness you are my shining light
Keep me always in thy sight
In doubt you are there to see me through
You give me confidence
That can only come from you
In despair you always comfort me
In shelter of your love I'll always be

Calm me with your Spirit

Lord calm me with your spirit
Fill me with your love
Still my anxious heart lord
With blessings from above
Let me know you love me each and every day
Lord always walk beside me
And be with me come what may
You are my strength and guide lord
My bright and shining light
You always fight for me lord
With your power and your might

Cherished and Blessed

I am cherished
And I am blessed
In my savior is eternal rest
I cannot comprehend
Your unconditional love
It flows from the throne of mercy above
Lord I believe you are there
To guide to comfort and to share
All your glory
And your grace
Lord one day I'll meet you
Face to face

As I Sit By The River

I think of my valleys
And mountains high
As I sit by the river
Watching it flow by
I think of the places I have been
And my heart is at peace
And my soul so serene
Lord you are the river that flows in me
The river of life and tranquility

Before I knew Your Holy Name

I lived in darkness
And in shame
Before I knew your holy name
There was no one to help me
Through trouble and sorrow
Only darkness around and no bright tomorrow
Then you came and set me free
And gave me a place in eternity
And all the darkness goes away
When I walk in your light
And in your name pray

Take a Stand

Come all you believers
Take a stand
With the word of the lord
Like a sword in your hand
Hold it up with shield of faith
And claim victory
In the name of the lord who set you free

Spiritually Minded

To be spiritually minded is to walk with lord
To read his word
And be in one accord
With the one who died
For you and me
In pain and sorrow he shed his blood
And he shed the tears
To wipe away
Our many fears
And fill our minds with his great love
And thank him
For our home above

Jesus Be With Me

In all that I do
Help me tell others'
All about you
May the Holy Spirit speak through me
To let them know he can set them free
Your love is pure
Unconditional and true
You can wash them clean
And make them new

In my father's house there are many mansions

In my fathers are many mansions
I know this is true
For Jesus told me so
And when my time on earth is over
To my mansion I will go
He will be there to welcome me
When I go to eternity
There be no more pain
And no more sorrow
For Jesus promised a bright tomorrow

Hold my hand Lord

Dear Lord Jesus holds my hand
For only you can understand
The hurt and pain I have been through
The I have shed when I am alone with you
You are my strength, my comfort, my guide
And io know you are always by my side
I give you honor
I give you praise
I will glorify you Jesus
Until the end of my days

Trust and believe

Trust and believe in all you have to do
And Jesus will come and live with you
He will tell you of the things he has done
He is Gods only blessed son
Read his words and say your prayers
Jesus will show you he really cares
He will wash away your sin
When you open the door and let him in

Don't Despair

When you feel lonely and in despair
Know that Jesus always there
Open the door and let him in
He will wash away your every sin
With Jesus forgiveness is very true
Because he loves and cares for you
He sent the Holy Spirit to be your guide
He will teach you
Jesus always by your side

His Hand in Mine

I was lying in an alley
With a bottle by my side
Filled with drugs and alcohol
I had no place to hide
People walked right by me
They didn't want to know
The broken wretch before them
With no place else to go
Suddenly I heard a voice
Call me by my name
Follow me into the light
Where there is no guilt and shame
Then something happened
My past was gone
My spirit was restored
And I walked out of that alley
With my hand in the hand
Of my Lord

My Healer

I'm shattered and I'm broken
As I come to You in prayer
Only You can mend me
As You take the time to care
You raise my spirit that is crushed
You heal my broken heart
You hold me in Your loving arms
And give me a new start

Shield of faith

Hold up the shield of faith when you pray
Put on your armor every day
Jesus is coming he's not far away
The trumpets are sounding one by one
They are preparing to fight with Gods son
Jesus is waiting for his father's command
To commence the battle that is at hand

Thankyou Jesus

Thankyou Jesus for my times of play
Thankyou Jesus for my time to pray
Thankyou Jesus for all you've done
Thankyou God for your precious son

The power of prayer

The power of prayer is an amazing thing
It heals the heart
And the broken wing
The lord gives me strength when I trust and pray
To conquer all things that come my way
I know he listens and he cares
And in his will he answers my prayers
I will praise his name in all that I do
Because only my lord
Can see me through
Philippians 4:13
I can do all things through
Christ that strengthens me
Love You Lord

Shine the light through me

Let the light shine forth from me
Help me guide the lost to thee
And show them and your mercy to
Showing them the light that leads to you

A Father and Son

A father and son have a bond of love
Whether near or far apart
When they are in this world or in heaven above
They live in each other's heart

Your dad lives in your memories
Of days gone by of all you used to do
So just know today he's not very far
He's always close to you

So today Dave
As you think of your dad
And all you used to do
Know that he is very near
And always thinking of you

Be my strength when I'm lonely Lord

My loved one has gone home to You
And I'm feeling so lonely now
Wrap Your arms around me
And please Lord show me how
To face the world outside my door
Without my loved one by my side
For in my weakness is Your strength
You've understood every time I've cried
You've always been there with me
Through the good times and the bad
You know my heart is broken Lord
And I'm feeling very sad
But I know we'll be reunited
And my loved one will be by my side
And Lord You've shown me the bottle
Of all the tears I've cried
So until these things come to pass
I'll dry my eyes and smile
Because the loneliness inside me
Will only last awhile

The Lords Prayer

Our Father who art in heaven
Glorified be Your Name
You are the one and only God
Who can take away our shame

Teach us that Your will be done
In heaven and on earth
Thank You that You taught us
The value of self worth

Give us this day our daily bread
To feed our body and our soul
Thank You for the food we eat
And Your Word that will make us whole

Father forgive us all our sins
Even the ones only You can see
And with a loving heart
Help me forgive those who sin against me

Lead us not into temptation
As it often comes our way
Remind us to pray in Jesus' Name
And not be led astray

For the power and the glory
And the kingdom is all Thine
Thank You Father for this mighty prayer
That was taught by Your Son divine

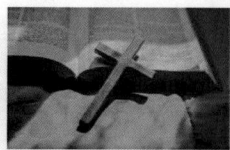

Wisdom

Lord gives me the wisdom
To know not to speak
But come to you and pray
Give me the wisdom to only speak
The words you would have me say
Lord holds my tongue
So I can speak the words you desire
For I know lord one spark from my tongue
Can become an uncontrollable fire
Just use my tongue to speak love lord
Whatever I may do
And mercy and compassion
Covered by the grace
That comes from you

Underneath your wing

Hide me lord under your wings
Give me a new song
That my heart sings
Put your feathers around me tight
Keep me always in your sight
For you're my all
And I love you so
And I will go wherever you go

Angels

When I lay in my bed at night
Dread darkness comes
As I turn off the light
I see many treasured things
Flickers of light from angels wings
I know my Jesus them there
To keep me safe in their heavenly care
And I can sleep in peace and love
Protected by angels from god above

Praise Glory and Honor

Angels in heaven praise your name
Your children on earth do the same
For you lord deserve the glory and praise
So, with the angels our voices we raise
And together with the angels above
We thank you and glorify you for your
Wondrous love

Happiness

Happiness is my special friend
He will love and teach me to the end
Happiness is my lord and guide
He's always by my side
Happiness is my father's son
Who said to his father his will be done
Happiness is knowing love
And eternal life in heaven above

Jesus will see me through

When pain and sorrow comes your way
Jesus will see you through each day
He will guide you with his loving hand
Because all your life has been already planned
So when the darkness hides the sun
Just tell our father his will be done
And he will make your dark days bright
So put your trust in gods own son
For with Jesus you'll see all
Your battles won

In the beginning

In the beginning our father did make
The entire world for our sake
He created the bird, flowers the trees
The sun and the moon for you and me
Then to finish his master plan
He formed from the dust the very first man
He breathed into his mouth
And then he formed the very first woman
The man's name was Adam
And the woman's eve
Then Satan moved in and they deceived by eating the fruit
From the forbidden tree
It was the beginning of sin for you and me
Then god came to the garden so he could walk
With Adam and Eve so they could talk
But when they saw him they tried to hide
They knew there and then that Satan had lied
They tried to cover themselves and their shame
They looked around for someone else to blame
That seems to be what we do today
When we don't know and run away
And we cannot face him when we've done something bad
Oh how we make our father sad
When he sees us running from his sight
Into the darkness and out of the light
Don't be like his first creation
Turn your back on Satan's temptation
Turn to Jesus our father's son,
And tell our father his will be done

There's power in Jesus name

When we go through tribulation
God will show us his salvation
Which he gives us through his son
Once we say thy will be done
He will wash away our sins and shame
When we pray in Jesus name
For Jesus bled and died for all
And he will always listen when we call
He rose again so we could be
For ever with him in eternity

Under Gods wings

When prosecution comes my way
And it's on every side
I go to the throne room of my god
And under his wings I hide
I know I am safe within his care
And he dries up all my tears
He whispers how I love you child
Go back and have no fears
For I am with you always
Not just here in heaven above
And when you are prosecuted
I will cover you with my love

Your Throne Room

When I'm feeling down and blue
And really don't know what to do
I lay my head upon your shoulder
And I feel all your compassion
From your throne above
I know you're with me wherever I walk
But it's in your throne room, I love to talk
And tell you all the things I've done
And praise and thank you for your son
You're my loving all who really cares
And listens to every one of my prayers
I feel so safe when I'm under your wing
And I can tell you anything
I know you've bottled all my tears
And you take away all my fears
I know you are with me
Through pain and sorrow
And I'll be back in your throne room tomorrow

My soul was lost

My soul was lost, I know not where
And at that time I did not care
I was running from God's shining light
I knew even then the wrong from the right.

I kept on going in all the wrong ways
There wasn't much to look forward to in those days.
I got up in the morning, then went to bed
With nothing in between except fear and dread
Of whatever was waiting the very next day.
Because in those days I didn't know how to pray
I didn't know I had a friend who would guide
My footsteps to the end.

I was too busy worrying and running around.
Then one day this friend I found
There He was just waiting for me
I said I love you, please set me free.

He lifted me up to the mountains high
And I could nearly touch the sky
Then the love inside me overflowed
When Jesus came and took the load.

The angels sang and the sun shone bright
That day I saw His shining light.
And now each day is bright and new
And with the love of Jesus I say, I love you.

Help Me Show My Friends

Father, help me show my friends
That they don't have to cry
For Jesus loved them all so much
That He did freely die.
And when they come to that point in life
Where there is no more to give
Help me show them that through His blood
They can go on and live
In that wonderful place that He has prepared
Where His children find rest for their souls
And their names are written before the Lamb
On that wonderful God made scroll.

The Gifts Of God

Why do we get so uptight today
With the gifts that Our Father gives?
Why can't we realise today
That the spirit within us lives?
And the spirit loves and cares
And wants us to
Use our gifts
With love that's true
God gives us gifts to share with others
t to put ourselves higher than our sisters and brothers
And not make them feel inferior
Or ourselves become superior
Let's remember we would not have
The gifts from God above
If we didn't know the Saviour,
and show others the Saviour's love.

As I Pass Through This World Lord

As I pass through this world, Lord
As the stars pass through the night
Let me shine just like the moon
Give me Your special light.

Father, let me be Your child
And listen to what You say
Keeping my eyes wide open
And in everything obey.

Slow me down when I start to run
And don't take time to see
The beautiful things that You create
The birds, the flowers, the tree.

The peace and love I thank You for
As each day starts a new
And for my life through Jesus
In eternity with You.

Many Religions

There are many religions in this world
Catholic, Baptist, Jew
Mormon, Jehovah Witness
Just to name a few.

If we took a little cut of each and everyone
Maybe we'd see more clearly
The love of Our Father's Son.

For Jesus is a religion
He's a person who really cares
And all our trials and problems
I know He gladly bears.

He's the spirit who dwells within us
He's the Father who made all things
He's the Son who lived and died for us
He's the Saviour of whom my heart sings.

He Grows With Me

I am only a little girl
and Jesus is my friend.
I know He loves me very much
and an angel He will send,
To live with me and guide me
Wherever I may go.
And Jesus will live in my heart
However big I grow.

Jesus My Brother

I have a brother I love dear
Who's always by my side.
He walks and talks along with me
And there's times when I've known he's cried.

He's cried for all his poor lost sheep
Who've strayed far from the flock.
And to believers they do laugh
And scorn and even mock.

But all my brother has to do
Is put His arms around them tight.
And they will never stray again
From His precious loving sight.

And all it takes is for us to care
Helping my brother with a prayer.

Be Prepared for an Angel

God sends His angels to us
In every kind of disguise
But you will know His angels
If You look through Jesus' eyes
Some need a hug
Some need a smile
Some need your love and care
And when you meet an angel
Take time to say a prayer

To See the Stars Shine Above

To see the stars shine above
To have someone to treasure and love
To watch the sun rise and set again
To have someone to share the rain

I can't live without your endless love
There is no doubt about it
It comes from above
I can't live without your endless smile
There's no doubt about it
It's there for awhile
I can't live without your endless sharing
There is no doubt about it
It's your way of caring

Resting on your shoulders

I rest my head on your shoulders of love
Wrapped in your arms on the throne above
You've known me lord since my day of birth
You've guided me in my journey on earth
Your always with me through laughter and pain
You pick me up again and again
I rest my head on your shoulders of love
In your throne room above

The Lord Understands

Our lord knows pain
And our lord knows sorrow
And all we have to do is borrow
Just a few moments of each day
To go to our lord and faithfully pray
Ask him for his love and care
Because he loves you and always be there
He will understand what's troubling you
And with your faith he'll pull you through
There is no greater pain to bare
Than the pain he suffered hanging there
Upon a cross for all to see
He loved his father and you plus me

Anointed Hands

Lord thank you for anointing my hands
I raise them to praise your name
Thank you for all the things you've done
Since in my life you've come
Teach me lord to use these hands
To only do your will?
For you know the plans you have for me
Lord help me fulfil all the blessings
You've placed in these hands
For I know now the purpose you have for me
To use these hands you've anointed
To write your poetry

Praise God In All You Do

Praise god in everything you do
Praise him for watching over you
Praise him when you're feeling down
Praise him for your heavenly crown
Praise him for always being there
Praise him for you're his loving care
Praise him for the things he's done
Praise him for his loving son
He is our father who truly saves
So lift your voice and give him praise

Ask For Forgiveness

There's the power of Satan that roams the Earth
Ready to take you from your time of birth
Don't give in to his hate and lies
For straight to Our Father's throne he flies.

He tells him of the things we've done
Ask for forgiveness in the Name Of The Son
And he will flee from the Father's throne
For Jesus is there protecting his own.

Teach Me How To Live

Please Jesus teach me how to live,
And share my love and always give
To anyone who needs a friend,
A smile, a hug and a prayer to mend
A broken home, a broken heart.
And show them they can be a part
Of a family who really cares,
And a Father who listens to all our prayers.

The Lord Is On Your Side

Don't sit down, get up and fight
The Lord is on your side.
There is no need to run away
And find a place to hide.

You're running in the dark you know
You'll never find the light.
Your life will never know the day
It will be as dark as night.

Let Jesus come into your life
He's right outside your door.
Open it wide and say 'come in'
And you will run no more.

All the dark you thought you had
Will quickly fade away.
When you see His shining light
And believe Him when you pray.

You'll have a friend who's always there
With all your battles won.
He is our blessed Saviour

God's wonderful loving Son.

The Face Of Jesus

When you're tired and weary
Of the troubles that arise,
Look into the face of Jesus,
And you will see His eyes
Are loving, warm and tender,
And His voice says I love you,
Cast on me your burdens
And I will see you through.
Don't wait till they get heavy,
And they seem too hard to bare,
Come to the foot of my cross,
And leave them with me there.

Happy times

Happy are the times with you
When joy comes to my heart
Happy are thoughts I have
Now I know we'll never part
For you live deep inside of me
You are my body, mind and soul
Thankyou Jesus for healing me
And making the broken pieces whole

Joseph's Dedication

Lord we dedicated to you this tiny little boy
Please give him all Your love, peace, happiness and joy
Give him strength to follow You in whatever he chooses to be
Open his eyes to all things Lord
On the path that leads to Thee
Lord, I pray that your strong arms
Will guide him through his days
And he will know You're always there
And in all things give You praise
Father, we cannot see ahead
For this tiny little boy
We only know You sent him
And with him comes great joy
We do humbly thank You
As we stand here and pray
Please help us guide him through his life
As a family this we pray.

The River

I see the river running by
It looks like the earth is having a cry.
Maybe it's the tears from all the pain
Of people who don't know Jesus' name.

I sit and I look and wonder why
All those people have to cry.
If they could open their eyes and see
The Saviour loves them as much as me.

For my tears were in the river too
And I was blind like some of you.
The I stopped and listened a while
About a man who went on trial.

He was found guilty of something he didn't do
Suffering all that shame for me and you.
He carried a cross down a long narrow road
And all our sins were his heavy load.

Not once did our Lord and Saviour complain
Because eternal life for us he'd gain.
Oh, how still the river flowed
When I put my feet on the long narrow road.
And I put my hand in the hands of a friend
Who will guide my footsteps to the end.

Thy Wonderous Love

Lord bless me with Thy wonderous love
Show me what can be done.

For I so love you Father
For sending us Your Son.
He came upon this earth one night
With all Your love and grace.
He came to lead us in the light
Until we see Him face to face.

What a precious Son he is
He never let you down.
Now he sits at your right hand
With the stars you made a crown.
To place upon His loving head
So, the angels all will know,
He's Your beloved Son Jesus Christ
To whom my life I owe.

Happiness

Happiness is always there
When you are by my side
You strengthen and protect me
You are my refuge and my guide
I love you so dearly
With a love that will always last
Because now my heart rejoices
You took away my past

When I'm alone

When I'm alone and going to cry
You are the only one
Who understands why?
Because you walked alone on earth
Please help me find my own self worth

 ### Rainbow

When there are tribulations, trials and sorrow
God shines through with a bright tomorrow
He places his rainbow in the sky
Whenever we ask him the reason why
He reminds us of his promise true
He gave a long time ago to me and you

Plan and Purpose

The plan and purpose I have for you
If you trust in me
I'll see you through
I will guide you with my love and care
For in your weakness, I'll be there
You are my child
And whatever life brings
You will soar with me on
Eagle's wings

Matthew 18:10

Lord I know it breaks Your heart
When a child is being abused
Sometimes they come from a broken home
Other times they're just being used
I pray You'll send each one of them
An angel from above
To cover and protect them
Because these children need all Your love
Let us be Your open arms
And give them Your comfort when they weep
For when a child has pains and hurts
The scars inside are very deep

Never Ending Story

You are so worthy
To be praised
You our Father
Of Honour and Glory
You are loving
Compassionate and true
And You wrote
A never ending story

I'm a little light for Jesus

I'm a little light for Jesus
He loves me this I know.
I opened up my heart to Him
And His love through me doth show.

I'm a little light for Jesus
I shine both night and day.
I ask You Lord to teach me
The right things I must say.

I'm a little light for Jesus
And I glow in the dark.
When I came to know my Lord
He put on me His mark.

He says He loves me dearly
For the things I say and do.
I'm a little light for Jesus
And You can be one too.

Multicoloured Angels

As I go to sleep each night
And close my eyes real tight
I can see the angels
On my left and right
They come in multicolours
With halos round their head
And as I sleep till morning
They guard me
Round my bed

Anointed Hands

Lord thank You for these anointed hands
I raise to praise Your Name
Thank You for the things You've done
Since in my life You came
Teach me Lord to use these hands
To only do Your will
For You know the plans You have for me
Lord help me to fulfill
And all the blessings You've placed in these hands
For I know now Your purpose for me
Is to use these hands You anointed
To constantly work for Thee

Guardian Angels

Pour on me Your Spirit Lord
Anoint me with Your love
Send angels down to guard me
From Your throne above
Place them on my left and right
To keep all harm away
Always right beside me
As I awake to each new day

My Rock

You are my rock, my strength, my gulde
Please keep me always by your side.
Give me happiness each day
And roll the clouds of dark away.

Just help me to be myself Oh Lord
Whatever I may do.
Remind me each and every day
My love and strength's in You.

Good Morning Jesus

Good morning Jesus is what I say
As I rise to greet each new day.
Thank you for keeping me safe through the night
And for posting Your angels on my left and right.

I know You'll guide me through this day
And be there to talk to, come what may.
Oh what a precious friend You are
You're my bright and shining morning star.

You And Me

God can make a rosebush
And God can make a tree
Why then should we not believe
That God made you and me.

He cultivates the rosebush
He shapes the strong tall tree
He gave His only son
To give life to you and me.

If I were a Bird

If I were a bird, I'd fly so high
I'd fly beyond the clear blue sky.
Then I would know that I would be
In a place we call eternity.

There I'd bow down before my Lord
For I know we're in one accord.
I love Him and he loves me
But I'm not a bird with wings you see.

God didn't make me a bird with wings
He gave me many other things
He gave me legs to walk His land
And I'll always be at His command.

He gave me a voice to say "I love you"
And a heart to know these words are true.
He gives me strength in times of need
Oh, Jesus is a friend indeed.

Lord, I don't need wings to fly
Just knowing that You're standing by,
Is enough to make my heart so light
I know I'm always in your sight.

Oh thank you Jesus for what I am
And for making me part of Your master plan
And for giving a new song that my heart sings
I'm just as free as a bird with wings.

Mould Me Lord

Mould me Lord and make of me
Whatever it is You want me to be
Hold my hand wherever I go
So Your precious love through me can flow
And people around can easily see
That I love You and You love me
You're a brother to me
A friend and a guide
And its' comforting to know
You're there by my side.

Lord Jesus How I Love Thee

Lord Jesus how I love Thee
I love Thee with all my heart
And with your hand in my hand
I know we'll never part

You keep me always safe
No matter what comes my way
And I know you'll always love me Lord
And I just want to say
Lord Jesus how I love Thee.

The Miracle Of Birth

The beauty of a sunset
The fragrance of a rose
The shade of a big oak tree
The river as it flows.

All these things would not exist
But for the hand of God
Even the bush and wildlife
Where man has never trod.

He made them all
And many other things
The fish that swim in the sea
And the birds with multicoloured wings

He made the Heavens and He made the Earth
But the greatest thing Our God created
Was the miracle of birth.

My Precious Daughter

God sent me an angel from above
A precious daughter for me to love
I want you to see I miss you so
From a child to a woman
I've watched you grow
And I am so very proud of you
For all that you say and do
And as I close my eyes each night
I pray God will keep you in His sight
You're a special child of His and mine
And you're covered by His love divine
So until you're in my arms again
And when we're not so far apart
May the angels guard and watch over you
For God knows the love of a mothers heart

You are so Worthy to be Praised

Angels in heaven
Praise Your Name
Your children on earth
Do the same
For You deserve
All Glory and Praise
You are our Father
So our voices we raise
And together with angels
Who sing above
We worship and thank You
For Your wondrous love

Flower In God's Garden

I'm a flower in God's garden
He planted me this I know
He waters me with love each day
And cares for me as I grow
I'm only a little bud right now
But I have made a start
For I love Jesus every day
And He lives within my heart
It might seem such a tiny place
For Jesus to live in
But as I grow he'll grow with me
And keep me free from sin
I'm a flower in God's garden
And God can plainly see
That I love Jesus with all my heart
And I know that He loves me.

I Love You So

Lord Jesus how I love You so
For the things you've done for me
You died so I might live again
For eternity with Thee.
You took away my many sins
And made me clean and whole
You made me clean in thought and mind
In body and in soul.
You died that I might be reborn
In Thy wondrous, precious Name
Oh, Jesus how I love Thee
Since in my life you came.

No Past

Happiness is always there
When You are by my side
You strengthen and protect me
You're my refuge and my guide
I love You oh so dearly
With a love that will always last
Because now my heart rejoices
You took away my past

I Give You My Life

I give You my life
I give You my love
And You give me a home
In heaven above
So please hold my hand
And hold on tight
And fill me with
Your power and might

You Understand

When I'm alone
And going to cry
You are the only one
Who understands why
Because You walked
Alone on earth
Please help me find my own self worth

Love God Your Father

Love God your Father with all your heart
And in everything give praise
For you never know when God will call
For you to close your days
Upon this earth where you've had your choice
Which path you'll walk upon
There's Satan with his greed and hate
And God with His loving Son.

There's no turning back once God has closed
The door of life on earth
You've freely walked the path you chose
From the time He gave you birth.
So don't close the door to life in your heart
Let Jesus come in and you'll be a part
Of a family who have eternal life in glory up above
Walking the paths with Jesus
Wrapped in His warmth and love.

How would we be?

There was a cross on a hill
Where our Lord Jesus died.
And if that cross was there today
Would we have stood and cried?
Or would we be like one of those
Who shouted "crucify"?
And stand and laugh and mock Him
When He knew to save us He must die.
How great He is, what love He shows,
And through the life He sacrificed, our life freely flows.

Thank You Lord For Me

Oh Lord there's people in this world
Who cannot walk or see
There's those who hunger every day
Oh, Thank you Lord for me.

I have two legs to walk your land
I have two eyes to see
I have my food everyday
Oh, thank you Lord for me.

I have a mouth and voice to laugh
And a soul that you set free.
I have two arms to hold on tight
Oh, thank you Lord for me.

I Feel So Great

I feel so great
I walk so straight
My eyes are open wide
And to You my Father I do bow
With greatest love and pride.
I thank you Father for Your son
The brother I do love
He died so we might live with Him
In glory up above
Jesus is my special friend
I know Him day by day
I walk with Him
I talk with Him
I hold hands with Him when I pray
Oh, Father how you mean so much
To all my family
And as You call us one by one
I know just where we'll be
And to you Jesus, please hold my hand
Don't ever let it go
And with You holding on so tight
Others will know, I know.

Australia Remember

The ship was swaying, and the sails were high
There wasn't a cloud to be seen in the sky
I stood on the deck looking out to sea
Wondering what this new land held for me

My wife and children were asleep below
The there were others we didn't know
They were the convicts crushed down in the hold
I think their story should be told

It was late at night when they came aboard
Their protests and cries were completely ignored
One was a child as old as my son
And I wondered what he could have possibly done

He looked at me with tears in his eyes
As I listened to his mother's cries
And the mother screamed out with fear and dread
"Please don't take my son, Take me instead."

"He only stole food for myself and his brother."
I closed my eyes and said a prayer for his mother
Then I was shaken back to reality
As the hatches banged down and they were no longer free

Continued on next page

And as I stand here with hope in my heart
I won't ever forget that they were a part
Of building the land that I am going to.
Australia, remember they're part of you.

I am the Murray

The willows bow before me and the gum trees line my banks,
    like soldiers in an army all standing in their ranks.
I've seen so many changes, there's been struggle, pain and tears
    and the hope of generations as I flow on through the years.

I've seen the gallant hearts of men as they pioneered this land
and their dreams become reality as the hardships they withstand.
They come from places far and wide and build along my banks,
where the gum trees and the willows stand like soldiers in their ranks.

I've carried the paddle steamers to towns and outback farms
and seen the strength of women with their babies in their arms.
They came with willing hearts and beside their menfolk they did stand
    Many buried their babies in this harsh and rugged land.

They walked together side by side through hunger, pain and sorrows
    for they had visions of greater days; they were the hope of all tomorrows.
and as night fell and the moon arose they stood upon my banks,
where the gum trees and the willows stand like soldiers in their ranks.

Continued on next page

As I twist and wind my way along this hot dry land
and the sun sets in the evening, I can understand
the hopes and dreams of men who came to tame this wild country,
with its rolling hills and barren plains and rivers just like me.

I am life to many creatures, the koala and the 'roo.
The laughing kookaburra and the crested cockatoo.
The fish that swim within me and the frogs upon my banks,
where the gum trees and the willows stand like soldiers in their ranks.

Australia My Land

The beauty of the sunset
The fragrance of a rose
The shade of a big oak tree
The river as it flows
The peace that's in the countryside
The surf, the sea, the sand.
A lovelier jewel you will not find
Australia, you're my land.

Reserve Us A Seat

The trials and problems of life we face
Only by God's love and grace
For without God's love, I fall to see
The light at the end of the dark for me.

Each problem that obstructs our road
Is willingly cleared when we give the load
To the one who carries all our care
And makes our burdens easy to bear

For who knows more about life on earth
Than our Lord Jesus Christ
Who had all the trials
From His time of birth.

It's such a joy to know that He's there
And the spirit moves in when we say a prayer
If we open our heart and believe

The spirit has asked, and we will receive
The answer to all of the prayers we pray
And out of the dark will come a bright day.

Bless me in my home Lord!

Bless me in my home Lord
Help me make it bright
Help me through my busy days
And give me peace at night.
You taught me how to pray Lord
For my home and family,
And when my home it quiet Lord
As a child I come to Thee,
To pray for patience and Your love,
To guide me through each day,
And give me strength
To see me through
Whatever may come my way.

Hear my Prayer

Hear my prayer
As I come to You in prayer
Hear me Father
For I know You really care
Pour on me Your Spirit
And lift my soul on high
Let me soar above my pain
Hold me when I cry
Hear me Father
When things in life go wrong
Hear me oh my Father
As I praise You with a song

One of a kind

When You look into my face
I pray that You will see
The love of Jesus
Shining from me
Don't look at my faults
They're easy to find
Just see me through God's eyes
I'm one of a kind.

Beacon of Light

Make me a beacon of Your love
That people can easily see
The light in the dark
So they are drawn
Oh Jesus please use me
Shine Your light upon me
Like a beacon in the night
Guiding everyone I meet
To Your everlasting light

Faith

Faith is a word we all should know
Ad through our faith our love should show
To our brothers and sisters who've never heard
That small but everything God sent word.

Faith is something you cannot buy
It's not something that's seen with the naked eye
It comes from the heart and the love that we show
To our Lord Jesus Christ
Wherever we go

So, if you have faith that's all you need
Whether it's as big as a mountain or as small as a seed.

The Foot of Your Throne

You fill me with Your Spirit
From Your glory up on high
Only You know when I'm happy
Only You know when I cry

I try so hard to do the things
That I know are so right
Please Lord, I love You oh so much
Keep my in Thy sight

Sometimes I come from beneath Thy wing
And get lost in a world of my own
Just guide me gently back again
To the foot of Thy heavenly throne

Hear My Father

Hear my father as I come in prayer
Hear my father for I know your there
Pour on me you spirit
And lift my soul high
Let me soar above my pain
Hold me when I cry

He'll See You Through

When pain and sorrow come our way
The Lord will see you through each day
He'll guide you with His loving hand
All your life has already been planned.

So when the darkness hides the sun
Just tell our Father His will be done
And He will make your dark days bright
He'll guide you with His shining light.

My Pen My Friend

The white blankness
You start to flow
Honesty is open
Insight you show
How do I repay such a trusting friend?
By continuing helping others
Through my pen

Robyn Ward

Sunlight Through The Cube

I see you in that glass cube
Sunlight hits all is revealed
To the side I move and there you are
More of you near and far
Sadness fills your bowed down faces
I reach my hand in all those places
Take it my friend and you shall find
The hand that you're holding will be mine

Robyn Ward

Look For The Butterflies

Mum at your side holding your hand
Speaking of heaven and angels so grand
God is around you and your spirit will rise
You can see love and such peace in your eyes
As you look at each other with content and a smile
You have memories of mum and you, her first child
Nurturing love, So natural and pure
Mum so wise as she speaks of your future
Holding you tight as you fall asleep
Knowing it's Jesus you'll soon meet
When you awake coming out of your dream
Saying it felt like I fell out of a tree and landed on a pillow
How true it seemed
Another day starts and your carer arrives
Hoping there's no trouble or strife
A personal friend that listens, laughs and cries
She would give you and mum a kiss goodbye
Then the banter begins with a ridgey didge
Someone would get a drink from the fridge
She speaks to us girls all through the day and says
Look for the butterflies as they pass your way
Love you

Robyn Ward

Love

Love is such a small word
For everything it says
It gets you through the hardest nights and the
Loneliest of days

It can reach out to all around you
And bring great peace of mind
It's a word that isn't easy
For some of us to find

And yet if we look to Jesus
And see what he has done
It's a word that God did give us
When He sacrificed his son

What greater love can someone show
Than to give his life for others
For you and me he gave His life
My sisters and my brothers

So let's open our hearts and wear a smile
And share this word around
For all of those that once were lost
With love, could now be found.

Create in me Your Spirit

Father create in me a spirit
That is strong, mature and new
Create in me a spirit
That gives all control to You
For You know I'm only human
And temptations come my way
Create in me Your Spirit
So, I'll not be led astray

Trust in Me

The plans and purpose
I have for you
If you trust in me
I'll see you through
I'll guide you with
My loving care
For in your weakness
I'll be there
You are my child
And whatever life brings
You will soar on eagles' wings with me

Sow Our Fathers Seeds

There are people we'll meet everyday
Who have great wants and needs.
The Father sends them to us
So that we may sow His seeds.

And if we sow those seeds with love
And show them that we care
Then I know Our Father will listen
When we go to Him in prayer.

But if we walk away from them
Because we're afraid to love,
Then how can we hope our prayers
Will be heard by God above.

So, share what God has given you
And make your life worthwhile,
Greet everyone who comes your way
With a loving caring smile.

He Grows With Me

I am only a little girl
And Jesus is my friend
I know He loves me very much
And an angel He will send

To live with me and guide me
Wherever I may go
And Jesus will live in my heart
However big I grow.

Life Is a Blessing

Life is a blessing
I gave to you
And no matter what comes
I'll see you through
For you are my child
And I am always there
Just talk to me
And I'll answer your prayer
And I know all that is good for you
And with my love
I'll see you through

Faith and Hope

Thankyou lord for faith and hope
For through these gifts
We can really cope
With anything that comes our way
Teach us not to go astray
Take us through Your refiner's fire
Lift our souls higher and higher
Sift the dross from our lives below
So, when we're ready
To You we'll go

I'm not Alone

Thank You Father I'm not alone
As I humbly come before Your throne
Your loving Son
Is holding my hand
As before You with me, He will stand
On that great and judgment day
He intercedes for me
When I pray
He is the shepherd who looks
After His sheep
So, before You Father
I know He'll keep
Me in His loving heavenly fold
Where I will never ever grow old

Praise

Praise God in everything you do
Praise Him for watching over you
Praise Him when you're feeling down
Praise him for your eternal crown
Praise Him for always being there
Praise Him for all His loving care
Praise Him for the things He's done
Praise Him for His loving Son
His is our God who truly saves
So, lift your hearts
And give Him all the praise

Death is just a whisper

Death is just a whisper
Of god saying child come home
I love you for the time you spent
Kneeling before my throne
And in my arms you cried your tears
I wiped them all away
I poured my love upon you
When I heard you pray
So come my child and be at peace for all eternity
You will live in the place I have prepared for you
And all your loved ones you will see

Butterfly

God created the butterfly
And painted its wings
He created the canary
Who whistles and sings
He created the flowers
The rivers, the tree
But his greatest creation
Was you and me

When I Go Don't Cry for Me

When I go don't cry for me
I'll open the door, and I will see
My Saviour coming down the road
And I will leave my heavy load
And I will run to Jesus' side
You see I haven't really died
I'm alive and well and happy here
I'll never shed another tear
For Jesus wiped them all away
And He did turn to me and say
"Well done my faithful servant true
I've been waiting here to welcome you"
He took me back along the road
Unto His loving heavenly fold
Where I saw things, I've never seen
Not in any place I've ever been
There are flowers and trees and people there
They walk around without a care
With bright and happy shining smiles
There are no worries or earthly trials
So, when I go don't cry for me
Just dry your eyes and smile for me
And love and always say you care
Then I will know that you will share
This wonderful place God's brought me to
And I'll wait on the road for you

Angel Wings (Scott's Song)

It hurts knowing
That I will never see you again
But I know you will still care about me
You're living in me
And as you fly to heaven
Your hands will turn to angel wings
We are all hurting
But you will always show us what to do
We will never forget
The fun and hard times we had
You're living in me
As you fly to heaven
My mind will turn to angel wings
It hurts knowing I'll never see you again
But I know that you will protect me from the pain
You're living in me
And as you fly to heaven
My face is stroked by angel wings
You're living in me
And as you fly to heaven
Your hands turn to angel wings
To protect me from harm
That may be around the corner
As you fly to heaven
And in my heart are angel wings
Love you big brother

By Aiden Bell

Wisdom And Knowledge

Lord give me the wisdom
To know when to speak
And when to pray
Give me the knowledge
To only speak
The words You would have me say
Lord cover my tongue
To speak the words, You desire
Guard it from being a spark
Becoming an uncontrollable fire
Use me to speak love
Wherever I go
So, others will know
The love that I know

Under Your Wing

Hide me Lord under Your wing
Give me a new song
I can sing
Put Your feathers
Around me tight
Keep me always
In Your sight
For You are my father and I love You so
And I will go wherever You go

Jesus Knows Our Needs

When You see someone in need
Don't turn and walk away
Show them the love of Jesus
Take their hands and pray
You don't need to know what's in their heart
For Jesus is already there
And when You speak, He'll hear You
For Your heart knows the power of prayer
And that someone's needs will all be met
Then all glory will go to our Lord
And we can thank and praise Him
That our hearts are in one accord

You Are Mine

Father, you came to me
When I needed You most
You revealed to me
Your Son and Holy Ghost
You told me of all the things above
You completely covered me with Your love
You changed my heart
From rain to sunshine
And now I am Yours
And You are mine

Troubled Waters

The waters rise and you can't think
Before you know it, you start to sink
Stretch out your hands, Jesus is there
He'll hold your hands and answer your prayer.

Never Ending Journey

I'm going on a journey
That God has promised me
Jesus paid for my ticket
When he set me free
He didn't even count the cost
Through all his pain and sorrow
He did it so I can have a bright tomorrow
Upon a cross at cavalry he was crucified
As he took my place
To wash away my many sins
And cover me with his grace
And my soul will worship as it sings
To the lord of lords
And the King of Kings

Don't Cry No More

When my heart is broken
And sorrow is at my door
Jesus wrapped me in His arms
And says "My child please cry no more
For I am, here to comfort you
And dry up all your tears
I will cover you with my love
And drive away your fears
Lean upon me when things go wrong
And in your weakness
I will make you strong
I am always with you
Walking by your side
Place your hands in mine
I am your friend and guide
When you're walking in the dark
And see a light ahead
It's Jesus carrying a lamp for you
To show you where to tread."

Do Unto Others

There are many in this world
Running to and fro
If they'd only run to Jesus
Then his loving care they'd know.
They turn to drugs and alcohol
And get trapped in a world of despair
They get banished to a cold grey land
There isn't much love in there.
They learn to fight and keep what's theirs
Behind grey prison walls
Their hearts grow cold to the Saviour's love
When on their names He calls.
Some cry their tears
Some hurt with shame
Some even take their lives
But what about their children,
their parents and their wives?
What place do they have in society
When their men are in that grey walled land
They certainly aren't top priority
Who gives them a loving hand?
We can if we open our hearts
And let the love of our Saviour flow through
For we must never ever, ever forget
That but for the grace of God
Those people could be you.

My Everything

Jesus is my everything
He gave me a new song
For me to sing
He pours his love
On me each day
He rejoices with me when I pray
He holds me in his loving arms
And takes away my fears
As he dries away my tears
So wherever I go
And no matter what I do
My Jesus is my everything
And He can be yours to

Watch and Pray

Watch and pray
In all that you do
Enter not into temptation
When it comes to you
Turn to me, I'm always there
I'll give you strength
When you give me a prayer
Don't give in to tempters lies
Just mention my name
And from you he flies

You are the way

You are the way
The truth and the life
Pour your blessing on me
To be a good wife
A good mother, sister and a friend to all
Let me hear your voice when you call
Anoint me with your wondrous love
Send down showers of blessings
From above

Patiently wait

Teach me to patiently wait lord
And to trust your guiding hand
To listen to you in the silence
Teach me to understand
Your perfect will, your steadfast love
When I am feeling all alone
Lift me up in your arms
To our father's heavenly throne

Early Morn

As I sit in the early morn
Waiting in the silence of the dawn
I reflect on you lord
And the things that you do
I'll sing your praise all day through
I'll put on the armor you gave to me
Shining so bright for all to see
Each day dawns
With new mercy and grace
One day I'll see your loving face
But right now, in your name
I have work to do
Telling people I meet
All about you

My Friend

Thankyou Jesus for being my friend
Thank you that you always lend
A hand in everything you do
Thankyou Jesus for being you

This is the day

This is the day that you have made
And as the sun rises
I come to you
Please cover me with grace and mercy to
Walk with me lord
In this brand new day
Listen to me lord when I pray
Thank you lord for All you have done
You are truly Gods beloved son

You are my Lord

You are my lord my savor true
I only want to follow you
When darkness comes
And I cannot see
Let your radiant light shine for me
Lord be there to catch me when I fall
You are my love and my all

Your Creation

You created the birds
The fish in the sea
You created the flowers
And the beautiful trees
You created the heavens
And the earth below
You send the rain
To all may grow
You created me to walk your land
And to always answer your command
So thank you father
For your creation
May all people bow down in every nation

Help me Lord

Help me lord to do what's right
Keep me always in thy sight
Remind me when I'm feeling down
Your promise to me of an eternal crown
You are my savior
Who lights my way, you always listen
When I pray
So when the dark clouds
Hide the sun
Remind me lord your will be done

To my sisters

God sent angels from heaven above
Beautiful sisters for me to love
There's nothing in life that we can't share
I love you so much for that you do
And for the times you've been there to see me through
Some of the things that have come my way
So, to you my sisters I just want to say
You're my angels sent from God above
For me to cherish and to love

You created all

When you made the heavens
And brought forth life on earth
When you created nature
And the miracle of birth
You made the sun
You made the moon
You created the stars above
You formed man and woman
And filled them with your love

When I am lonely

When I am lonely
I'll turn to you
Because I know you'll see me through
You've wiped away my heartfelt tears
That I've cried throughout the years
You held me in the palm of your hand
And when I fall you help me stand
In many ways I will worship you
Until the end of my days

Be still my child

Be still my child
Come take my hand
Give me your burdens I understand
By my Holy Spirit, I'll see you through
Anything that is hurting you
I know your love
And I know your pain
I've seen your tears
Again, and again
So be still my child and take my hand
For I can only understand

Home to rest

Soon I'll be home
Among the blessed
When Jesus comes and gives me rest
He will take me to my home above
Where there is peace and joy
Also unconditional love
No more pain
And no more sorrow
No more yesterday
No more tomorrow
I will stand in presence of my king
For he is my God
My everything

Take my hand

Dear Lord Jesus take my hand
When people around me misunderstand
Some of the things I say and do
As I worship and glorify only you
Fill my body, spirit and mind
For you made me to be Lord
One of a kind

Become my child

Become my child and take my hand
Your heartache and pain I understand
Your loneliness' and sorrow
Your tears I see
So, become my child
And sit with me
I'll give you strength to face each day
And peace in your heart come what may
So, come my child
I am right by your side
And in your heart, I will abide

Bless me today Lord

Bless me today lord
Teach me thy way
Anoint me with grace lord
For the rest of my days
Let me always be ready in all that I do
To find your lost souls, and lead them to you
You are my strength lord
My savior and guide
And as I go on my way lord
Your right by my side
I don't have to see you
To that you're there
I love and believe
That you always care

Sermon On The Mount

Walking in a valley
Looking at the mountains
Just ahead
You come into my mind
And into my soul
With the words
That You have said
You gave us many promises
Through the sermon
On the Mount
And more and more
To go with them
Much more than
We can count

Jesus Takes Our Burden

When you are weary
And heavily burdened
Jesus will take the load
He's our gentle Sheppard
We are safe
Within his fold
He is the son of God
The prince of peace
And his love for us will never cease
So whatever burdens you have today
Give it to Jesus
When you pray

Water of life

To God I am a strong oak tree
My roots grow deeper
As He waters me
And the water He gives
Is in His Word
Where He teaches me
All the things that occurred
From the time of creation
Until the time of the end
When Jesus and His angels
God will send
And all of those
Who after righteousness thirst
Jesus and His angels
Will take them first

He walks with me

Jesus walks with me and talks with me
He tells me that he cares
He listens to my every word
When I say my prayers
And if I fall
He'll be right by my side
And under his wings
I will hide
For there it is safe
And he dries my tears
He takes away all my fears
And then he puts me down on solid ground
And his light will shine all around
And I can talk to him again
He took away all my pain

Angels

Angels encamp around me
They come from God above
They show me not to fear
I am covered with their love
They can teach me understanding
They teach me to be wise
They show me that I'm worthy
In my father's eyes

Just Suppose

Just suppose God closed His eyes
And never listened to our cries
Where would we go, what would we do
Could you really rely on you?

Suppose He never turned on the sun
Suppose the rivers didn't run
Could you make light to make things grow
Or could you make the waters flow?

Suppose the father of all creation
Left you in the hands of Satan's temptation
What chance do you think you'd have to live
If His love, He didn't give?

Suppose God gave up the way we do
And didn't help and love us through
All our times of trial and sorrow
Suppose God didn't make tomorrow?

Suppose He went on strike today
Could you this loving God portray
Would you give up your only son
So, others' lives could be won?

I am sure you couldn't and
Neither could I
So, let's stop supposing and asking Him why
For in faith, we know He'll always be there
For whom but our God could answer a prayer?

Reach Out To Jesus

Reach out to Jesus
He'll see you through
For he is always there
Reaching out to you
He will guide you
With his love and care
He listens to your every prayer
With his arms out stretched
And unconditional love
He will guide your soul to heaven above
So when you are feeling down an low
Reach out for Jesus for he will always know

Speak to me my child

Speak to me my child I'm your father who really cares
Speak to me my child I will listen to your prayers
Know I love you dearly and always there for you
Speak to me my child and I will see you though

Give him The Glory

Give God the glory
For creating all things
He is the Lord of lords
And King of kings
Give him praise for all he has done
Sharing his love by sending his son
He came down from heaven above
To show us
God's unconditional love
A savior to take away all our sin
And the Holy Spirit to dwell within
So give him glory
And give him praise
He's the God almighty
The ancient of days

Jesus be with me

Jesus be with me in all that I do
Help me tell others all about you
May the Holy Spirit speak through me
To let them know Jesus can set them free
Your love is pure unconditional and true
You can wash them clean and make them new

The gospel of love

Go ye into all the world
And teach the gospel of love
Glorify the saviour who lives in heaven above
Teach the people you meet every day about Gods beloved son
And when they come to know him, their spirits will as one
Have nailed him to a rugged cross
On a hill at cavalry where he knows only pain
So, our spirits could be set free
So, glorify the father
And glorify the son
Glorify the Holy Spirit
For they are three in one

Treasures in Heaven

Do not seek the world and its pleasures
And I will give you the treasures
I have stored in heaven for thee
For you are worthy to take your place in paradise with me
You praised and glorified my name
And your reward from me is eternity

Communion

The table was set and our Lord sat down
And he said to His disciples there
"Come eat the bread and drink the wine
So, all of you may share
My body and my blood this day
For I know what I must do
There's one who'll betray Me in this room Yes, it is one of you"
They all looked up in dismay and despair
And they each said, "Oh, Lord Is It?"
And Jesus said my Father knows
So, let's not spend time asking why

Man And Wife

When You made the heavens
And bought forth life on earth
When You gave us nature
And the miracle of birth

You made the sun
You made the moon
You made the stars above
You made man and a wife
And filled them with Your everlasting love

Poem Of Communion

The love or Jesus is a wonderful love
It is total and instant and true
His love is unselfish, unconditional, warm
His love is for me and you.
He carried a cross down a long narrow road
To a hill where He knew only pain
And the people look up to our crucified Lord
With hearts that were selfish and vain.

They shouted abuse
And they scorned and they mocked
And they laughed "there's the King of the Jews"
But not once did your heart surrender that love
And not once did your heart accuse.

Lord Jesus on this our communion night
As we come to Your table and You
Please help us to have forgiving hearts
And a love so unselfish and true.

Thank You For Making Me

Thank you, Lord, for making me
For giving me eyes that I might see
Your beautiful world that's all around
For the flowers and trees
That grow from the ground.

For my heart that says "I love you Lord"
And in You have all my treasures stored
For my legs that will always walk Your way
For my mouth and voice that I might pray.

For my arms and hands that hold on tight
And they always come together Lord
When its time to say goodnight.
And thank You for every part of me
And for my soul that You set free

www.ingramcontent.com/pod-product-compliance
Lightning Source LLC
Chambersburg PA
CBRC091204070526
44583CB00011B/198